Existing Music

Also by Nick Thran:

If It Gets Quiet Later On, I Will Make a Display
Mayor Snow
Earworm
Every Inadequate Name

POEMS BY

NICK THRAN

NIGHTWOOD EDITIONS

2025

Copyright © Nick Thran, 2025

1 2 3 4 5 — 29 28 27 26 25

ALL RIGHTS RESERVED. No part of this publication may be reproduced, stored in a retrieval system or transmitted, in any form or by any means, without prior permission of the publisher or, in the case of photocopying or other reprographic copying, a licence from Access Copyright, the Canadian Copyright Licensing Agency, www.accesscopyright.ca, info@accesscopyright.ca.

Nightwood Editions
P.O. Box 1779
Gibsons, BC V0N 1V0
Canada
www.nightwoodeditions.com

COVER DESIGN: Natalie Olsen
TYPOGRAPHY: Rafael Chimicatti

Nightwood Editions acknowledges the support of the Canada Council for the Arts, the Government of Canada, and the Province of British Columbia through the BC Arts Council.

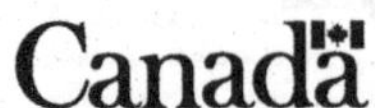

Canada Council for the Arts Conseil des Arts du Canada

This book has been printed on 100% post-consumer recycled paper.

Printed and bound in Canada.

LIBRARY AND ARCHIVES CANADA CATALOGUING IN PUBLICATION

Title: Existing music / poems by Nick Thran.
Names: Thran, Nick, 1980- author.
Identifiers: Canadiana (print) 20250121239 | Canadiana (ebook) 20250121255 | ISBN 9780889714861 (softcover) | ISBN 9780889714878 (EPUB)
Subjects: LCGFT: Poetry.
Classification: LCC PS8639.H73 E95 2025 | DDC C811/.6—dc23

For Ruth Roach Pierson (1938–2024)

CONTENTS

CONTENTS

TONE ROW

Is there anything better than arriving
an entire day before your meeting
and walking around Toronto in the rain?

Better than stopping at a couple of cafés to drink coffee
and read a novel about walking around in the rain
in Tokyo? A novel you can easily finish

in one afternoon, if no one talks to you,
if you clear your schedule and commit
to not fantasizing about the lives of anyone

in your peripheral vision, anyone casting a glance
when you look up from your cup, anyone
who might then become the kind of person

you'd feel compelled to try to portray
in a much longer novel. Is there anything better
than steam and rain, and the sound of the pages flipping,

and thinking about calling your mother
because the protagonist is walking
with *her* mother through Tokyo's streets?

Rainy day. Untranslatable noises outside. Walking
with this mother you do not yet know, who is not yet
here in the ways we mean when we say *that's her*.

Is there anything better than being a total baby
in a café in Toronto, and reading a novel before
you've learned to read? Than taking your own hand

like a child's, like a character in a novel,
and reading the title aloud to yourself,
which is the same title as this poem,

and it's COLD ENOUGH FOR SNOW.

A DAVID CLOUD BERMAN WEDDING DANCE

That idiom,
to take the floor.

That marriage
between dance and speech.

And "Tennessee"'s messed-up
opening warble,

how it takes a little time
to become a passably upbeat tune.

But eventually, aunts did
begin lowering their eyebrows;

the nephew's wooden arms
started making real boy moves.

Among the loves that night,
we loved their trust.

When we remember them,
we remember you.

OBLIQUE MOTION, METAVERSE

I found a handgun in the glove compartment.

Thank goodness there was also a cigar, a lighter
and a bottle of wine. I lit the cigar
with a hand that was mine
but did not move like mine.

I drank the whole bottle
and it tasted like nothing at all.

Yet it gave me a minute to consider my options.
Open the door, and risk being captured.
Maybe play around more with the ticking bomb
I'd just recently diffused.

To kill a bit more time,
I smashed the empty bottle against the passenger-side floor.
Put two bullets through the driver's side window,
which triggered a mysterious gas leak, a loud alarm.

My goal was to drive the car off the moving plane
and I was failing. I could hear my cousin's voice
offering strategies from another realm, strategies
difficult to discern, easy to curse—that is,
until the cargo door opened,
and the car,
and the glass,
and the man
in a suit made of pixels

who was meant to be me fell out of the plane
to where no one could reach him—
                                                    an Icarus, maybe,
if Icarus could have just shouted, "Pause."

SUBITO

A compact sedan full of teenagers overtakes
his eighteen-wheeler on the right.

Three thousand pounds of Greek yogurt
bound for Des Moines remain chilled in the back.

Clean cabin, smell of that rear-view air
freshener vanilla that does not last. Thus far,

not an unusual drive. Two yearlong tours overseas,
twelve more here at home with a latent rage—

an unpaid instrument of war. Vetch in ditches,
signs promising Wi-Fi and clean rooms.

The dashboard dancer broke down in tears
mid-dance, under the vanilla spruce.

Bodies and other truths that blaring
his horn at the road would never change—

nor would the Stones on repeat, "Wild Horses"
screaming at him from that faraway place in the dash.

NATURAL NOTES

Sad music thrives in a drive-through province.

A long moody sax solo
at Sappyfest in Sackville
                                        thrives.

Sad music thrives among lupins
                                        in the empty lot
where the Begbie place was razed,

it thrives among milkweeds,
the confetti of rusty Alpine,

it thrives when you hold
your phone up to the ghost door

while they practise their saddest one
so that somebody elsewhere
                                        can hear.

CERRITOS, CA, 1991 (PASTORALE)

That year we had a backyard with a swimming pool,
a wide lawn spotted with Max's shits,
shits mixed up with couch stuffing, lost earrings, crayons.

Only trouble I got in at school was for writing
with a mechanical pencil that looked like a syringe.
Only time I was afraid that year was when my friend

brought his older brother's gun downstairs to point at us
while we played *Battletoads* on his Nintendo.
Only time I remember being taken aback was passing

by the guns and ammo store near our local mall:
Back to School Sale on the window in big comic lettering.
Christmas, I wanted to close all the curtains and leave

the air conditioning on. I could hold my breath in the pool
for a long time. Open my eyes wide, in spite of the chlorine.
Max ate slippers, action figures. Fed him every day myself,

why on earth was he always so hungry? The power plant
where Dad worked had to be shut down for a week
to shoot a scene for *Terminator 2*, starring the future

governor. End of year, a group of employees threw
Dad a going-away party, gave him a thank-you plaque
for treating everyone as equals. That made me proud.

Rewards for what should be protocol now make me angry.
Meanwhile, out walking Max, Mom stole a single lemon
from a branch growing over the neighbour's fence.

I was sure she had done something wrong.
She'd done no wrong.
But it felt so good to be sure that I never forgave her.

HERMETIC FABRIC

As the idea of "taking a beat" expanded,
diehards let loose to obsessing . . .

First thoughts were hard drugs
or a sudden religious conversion.

But then considering that single, blissful
online picture from an emu farm

(location undisclosed) above their defence
of something dubbed "the sonic proletariat,"

it almost seemed possible to predict the dawn
of a new album's thematic directions.

The newborn twins were unexpected.
More expected, the experimental label,

whose six-month existence added maybe
three new bands to the lexicon,

three brief diversions the ears could hold.
When the coffee shop/dispensary

in the polyethylene district opened,
we thought maybe a guitar in the corner

and a room of goodwill might unlock
what was never really present

in their dry autobiographical novel
(set, as it was, mostly in childhood,

all descriptions of full moons,
stamp books, the wind's percussion

on the rickety outhouse door).
Too many of us contributed the cost

of a pint to a doomed-
from-the-outset fringe campaign,

even after they abandoned
what was known for a while

as the Abandoned Cannery Project,
a place of perfect acoustics

for the refusal of something.
But the refusal of what?

A Nordic word, perhaps.
Something trendy to look up

if or as soon as we ever
wake from this long, dreamy nap.

BAKERS AT DAWN

Each day she'd get up earlier. Drink tea,
collect her thoughts. The dough of the sun

began to thicken through the trees.
Hungry for more of the morning

she rose. She wanted to see the mouse
pirouette with confidence over

the darkened auditorium floor, wanted
to really *know* the snowy owl. Earlier

she rose, walking backwards through
the night. Walking backwards through

our dreams. Through last night's dinner
she'd wield a roll, drunk on the clarity

of time moving backwards, the stillness, new,
within herself. *I know where we get*

this bread, she'd say,
I know where we get this bread.

TONE ROW

After all those years of his tough-guy posturing,

I will remember my father's father hovering
over his transparent box of pills
as though admiring some kind
of extravagant bracelet.

And the delight that he took,
at the expense of other kinds of talk,
in describing what each small jewel was meant to do
to the various parts of his body.

And how my own father, being generous, just let him go on.
Then the mischievous look he bestowed

upon me driving home, and the glint on the sea.
And how we'd each remain bound to the other's wrist,

as we listened to some crooner
put coins in the waves,

to some Las Vegas glitz
that gets even the old gangsters smiling.

WOODWIND

The cedar's removal required a shovel,
but also shears, a handsaw,
larger shears,
and a pick and an axe
and a sledgehammer.

A twenty-minute video tutorial
from an Australian self-sufficiency guru
with bag-of-onions arms.

Five hours of exertion
over three afternoons.

A few more thoughts about the "o"
that rings a "root" to "rot."

Freudian imagery.
The willful dismissal
of a novel that had argued persuasively
for the sentience of forest floors.

The neighbours' slow claps
behind curtains.

The murder of crows
in the comments
quieting down.

A rest in the dirt.
Asleep in the dirt.

As close as I've been
to God's ear.

BETTER THAN IT SOUNDS IN REAL LIFE

I too was employed as a Foley artist.
Fist fighting with a boiled chicken,
frantically chopping a red cabbage,
running in place on a concrete pit
sprinkled with broken plates.

A good day was kneading cornflowers
inside of a pillowcase. A bad day
was running in place in the river pit,
eyes on the monitor, on a fake Paris street,

while the voice from the booth said, *Dance*
with your lips on the backs of your hands,
and I danced—
under a moon that played me
in the movies.

C/G

I was butchering a Big Thief song
on a green ukulele. Their song
about the infinite nature of potatoes.

It was a toy ukulele,
too small for my hands.
But I packed it around the house for a couple of years—

light as a leaf and easy to learn.
I love Big Thief.
Particularly their lead singer,

Adrianne Lenker. You can hear
late diner coffees with John Prine in her voice,
the blades of Joni Mitchell's ice skates.

Once a journalist asked Adrianne what records
she grew up listening to as a child
and she answered, *I was listening*

to my parents. I was listening to bugs
and the furniture in our house.
You can hear this listening in her voice.

(Could be what allows her to write
such beautiful songs about potatoes.)
When I moved on from the green ukulele

to guitar I learned more Big Thief songs.
Adrianne loves using this C/G chord,
in the slow stuff as well as the howlers.

Her songs are often just three chords,
generous with space for beginners like me
to feel around notes for their edges.

I still hide my voice when I play guitar,
but with her songs I dig inward,
sing me-seeming vocals.

Have you ever seen potatoes growing
in a field? Above ground they make these
gorgeous flowers. Have you ever taken

a family trip to Potato World?
We shot potato guns. Studied a wall chart
of the common potato deformations.

Ate heaping plates of fries.
Although I far prefer Big Thief,
I let the kids listen to Taylor Swift

on the way back home. I wasn't really listening
to Taylor Swift. I was listening
to the kids in the backseat singing

what they love to sing. The difference
has nothing to do with taste.
Later that fall, I was practising

Big Thief's "Change" in the kitchen
when my visiting mother surprised me,
knew the words, started singing along.

So much of what I love are things
that would have mortified me once.
I try to describe them

to my mother by letting her sing
in my kitchen without interruption.
I try to describe them in a plain-spoken poem,

a middle-aged amateur inventing a journalist
to give an interview nobody asked for.
I was listening to my parents.

I was listening to the potatoes in the fields,
their powdery scab, silver scurf,
verticillium wilt and late blight.

The flowers. The space around the chords.
To my mother and I singing
in the same field. "The secret of the quiet night."

THE MINIM

First off,
slow.

Slightly less slow
than adagio slow.

A walking
pace.

The first half
of a phrase.

An equal, tender
temperament.

Small metal touchers
striking the strings.

Demi-
semi-
quaver.

Don't deviate.
Don't link.

Don't go for the usual . . .

Don't go.

We're trying to establish a tone.

If the text refers
to ascent or descent,
the music does likewise.

If the text refers
to collecting money
it's probably time
to be true.

The theatrical
lute-playing
low male voice.

Vigorous chamber.
Frivolous room.

No more a dance
than a ballad.

Short, operatic
outdoor performance—

unaccompanied

(which should not be mistaken
for free).

Now a fugue sustained
for two performers.

A small coin.

　　　　A skittle.

But two equal subjects.

Two equal notes.

Daily,
despite the name,
the quaver, the electric guitar,
the microphone, the amplifier,
the repertory of computer music,
the meantime, the lip positions,
the pitch difference,
the illustrated passages,
the acts, the first
and second subjects,
the improvising,
the expressive content

despite *all that*

(which is obviously a part
of the score).

It is safe to say that numerous glee clubs exist.

Butterfly wings
never close.

Or they close
on Wednesdays only.

Even the ferns
need breaks.

Even grace notes
in groups.

Felicitations,
Europeans!
You did it.
You got the gigue.

A small private orchestra
is hard to define. It's the most remote line
of the manual. Not a melody at all,

but a series of ever-changing
colours in the cafés,
in the bathysphere—

fine print
in the peppermint tea.

The partner is of importance.

You want a partner.

They correspond.

A partner is some person
living or dead.

It is the end
of your isolated masterpiece.

Then text itself tends to become
unimportant,

although most partners
have made use of the form.

Try to keep pace
with the night animals.

Gloomy moon dance,
sticks and leaves.

"Song-like."

Never the noun.

The noun
implies a poem.

Then the quality of the spectacle
overshadows the text.

By "text"
I do not mean "partner."

Perhaps others around you play.

Perhaps they have never been born.

How did we find the dock,
paddling
without any lights

after drinking so much
of the lake,
of the lake,
of the lake . . .

from those comically large
glass jars?

A promising cable broke
mid-truth.

On a wave
or in the clock:

a summer,
a sunrise.

A common country
fiddle.

The whole note,
written.

The wooden surface.

Simply. Always.
Without.

A voice has its own piston
or rotary mechanism.

When the ordinary valves are used,
a voice has its own moss and pitch.

A voice combs its own wolf.

Arithmetic, geometry.
Music, astronomy.

Four instruments and a live trout
is five instruments.

Five notes,
five beats.

Play them "as-you-please."

Praise a mathematical term for existing.
Praise an alternative name for suite.

A brisk display
of existing music!

Little by little.
Next, next, next.

Degrees of sliding
between a solo
and a sequence.

Praise what is not quite smoothly joined.

Any piece with after-the-dance connections
begins, like charity should,
at home.

The piece will appear
for some time yet.

With its hothouse exoticism.
With its deliberate simplicity.

Like an avocado plant thriving
in the bay window,

with an almost inaudible,
subtle shade of Frog.

Seven planets.

The outline of a dog
on a grey carpet.

Floor damp for days
with durations of notes
and rests,

with the dog-
shaped cloud,

with the art
of using chords.

TWO ROOMS

SMALL TALK

Might have taken a snow day, but I like
opening the bookstore. Even those heavy-legged

steps there. Order a takeaway coffee, extra hot,
so after I shovel the sidewalk, put out the OPEN sign,

the cup will still be warm. Flick on the switches
for five afternoon hours of indoor light

in which I see nine customers,
sell four greeting cards, one collection

of personal essays, one YA novel, one self-
help book about getting rid of the habits

"that minimize the self." I love making the themed
(albeit only broadly associative) tabletop

displays. This one, called "Small Talk," includes
a book about the life of cells, something about knitting

"mini cosmos," the history of the mosquito,
the *Little Book of Word Origins* . . . The coffee is

still warm. I add a book about designing terrariums,
a discussion of "micro-trends," a debut work of fiction

called *That Tiny Life*.
I mentally compose this micro-fiction

where a cup of coffee stays warm for an entire day
and the protagonist tells this to everyone

who comes into the store. Workshop the plot
by snow shovel blade with a curious pigeon

who explains they come from a great line
of messengers, is out of work but still alive

by the grace of the smokestacks piping
from the tops of the buildings

as heat reads its shivering wings.
Exchange tips about kicking the nicotine habit,

what the gentlest kinds of road salt are—
the coffee is still warm.

Meanwhile Kalpna is constructing paper swans
for a window on Queen Street. Eiko,

after a long flight back from Kyoto,
is reading a poem about jetlag in an overstuffed chair

at the Community Bookstore on Seventh Ave.
John is stacking copies of the *BAKKA Anthology*

on a table on Harbord Street, in the store named
for "the weeper who mourns for all mankind."

Meaghan phones businesses around Ste-Catherine St.
to see who might repair the Argo's shattered glass.

Hsiang guards the tower full of books
described as "near and far at the same time"

in a poem by Jorge, who, according to Alberto,
ordered bland food at supper so the meal

would not distract the diners from the talk.
I love the visible edges of the tables,

the shelves. Try to cultivate an understanding
of the movements of a browser's voice and eyes,

when it's time to stop talking,
to leave them wandering, to rearrange

my own voice in accordance with new arrivals,
cold coffee, with the sun going down every day

like a grand idea put off as evening sorts out the stars
from streetlights, snow from the moving cars.

OH

I can hear it now as clear as day.
I was in the attic, trying to shave
something clear and concise
from a florid English translation
of a poem by José Hierro.
Nowhere near fluent in Spanish,
but having sense, I thought,
for the cadence of a line.

So I was taking great liberties,
doing what the poet Steven Heighton called
approximations, meant to excuse
inevitable monolingual errors in order
to establish an understanding between two poets
who might not otherwise speak.

You and I had recently moved into that attic,
painted the plum-coloured cloud pattern
in simple eggshell white.

Two rooms. Cheap rent.
A house of friends. I would get up early
to sit for a while at your desk
(the one by the window)
before you woke up,
borrow a bit of the morning light.

And my approximation was going so well,
I was feeling something akin to possession
I was *skinning the scent from the clouds,*
was *putting cold teeth into our flesh.*

I don't think that I heard your steps,
or felt your hand, but I heard your *Oh*
as you read over my shoulder. *Oh,*
you said, and then my name,
thinking I'd written the words on the screen.

Of course, right then—*no es mío*—
I came clean.

But I'd raid and bend and recompose
to recreate that place,

that second room where I could live,
even if it was not mine.

PORT OF CALL

One catches a lot of stray facts at the bookstore.

Seagulls in the air
and driftwood on the water's surface
are two indicators to the survivors of shipwrecks
that they may be close to land.

This man making his way
toward the cash desk is about to repeat
his story about a baseball game he saw in '86
before ordering two or three books about nautical disasters
that he rarely returns to buy.

Nevertheless, a transaction of sorts
occurs. And occasionally his eyes
seem to snag a flyball,
maybe his own last name scrawled
on the folded-over paper
(fastened to the book by a rubber band)
up there on the hold shelf,
one letter from the book's title
peeking from each end of the slip
and shining from the spine.

You fill out his new order. Yes,
we'll hold *The Ice Master*
for a couple more weeks.

He leaves. Others skim the shelves,
make purchases. After close,
boxes of unread books to return
are docked in neat rows, at the rear of the store.
And, though you don't often read poems,
the last line of one raises a hand:

before the real tears start flooding our eyes.

THE MUSIC OF OTHER WAVES

This other water:
        murky and coppery red.

The shape-shifting stains
        on a sea monster's teeth,
the miasmic wash
        of a sea monster's breath.

What emerged at the crest of a wave
        or in the valley that followed a wave
or at the crest of the wave
        after that.

The clock next to the log
        has sunk. The log
has sunk. The sun on deck is less
        a summer's morn
and more like a diagnosis.

Had they chased them far
        enough from shore?
Is to love this smeared image
        a morbid love?

Why cast their eyes
        on a sunrise like this?

Because otherwise only
        a monster does.

LUKA DONČIĆ

Sometimes I remember being able to distinguish
my best friend's footsteps
from the defence's oncoming footsteps
and throwing the ball over my shoulder
blind—
the game develops
I oscillate between extremes
of total isolation and hyper-connection
Sometimes I run through the forest listening to the forest
Sometimes my old friends text me links to songs
with those drums those drums those drums we like
I go to the forest I go to the clearing
Sometimes the line *the polyglot*
choreography of urban sidewalks runs through
my mind sometimes I find a little space
in the forest where light falls through leaves I think
God or Luka Dončić
pass the ball sometimes
the oncoming footsteps reach me
I'm devoured by foxes
I'm in the clearing thinking
I'm too young to be so tired
Sometimes a bird appears
out of the corner of something for which
I don't have words
and so I say my eyes

CLOUDS ON A DRIVE

Part burnt conifers, part salmon bellies.
                    The intersection where
ten lanes converge on a dog's breakfast
has been dug up. A cone. Another cone.
                    A cone. River that,
                    albeit beautiful to behold,
means we've gone too far.
                    Long curve back
                    towards downtown.
                    Summer rerun of *Ideas,*
                    a loud Irish jug band
in the bandshell serenading
the field of box-store folding chairs. Pause
                    at a green light,
                    the driver ahead in a smartphone bow
holding up the lane. Bit of excess speed
through a stretch of colonial homes where the sprinklers
sing in that Agee-an, *A Death in the Family* way.
                    But we weren't really late.
                    We couldn't be late.
We were just seeing the clouds from all sides.

YOUR BIRTHDAY IS OUR BIRTHDAY

Everyone remembers the nightmare of being born,
the raging maelstrom of turning one
and the emotional meat-grinder of turning two.

Or the abject terror upon waking
that first morning of our sixth year,
peeling the curtains like some awful scab

as parents' footsteps down the hall
mix with that bone-chilling, barely whispered
Happy Birthday song.

It's terrifying, turning ten—

so many vultures. And there's the dumpster fire
of fourteen. The crocodile aquarium of twenty-one.
The pain at twenty-five we must not name. And yet,

I've said nothing at all of the ghost rave of thirty-three
the quivering stem of fifty-eight, or even the lonely
moonlit loon of seventy-five,

out there on the dark water
of the years to come,
who calls and calls and calls.

Happy birthday! As per uszh
stay three metres away from the nearest balloon.

Nobody ordered a sad clown
but alas, he is here,
hunched by the punch bowl,
with bells on.

I could hear her gently lift the needle off the record, Prine's *Souvenirs* coming to a stop.

Now the silence in the house, to which we'd grown so accustomed, was starting to solo: rain; waves; cutlery crisscrossing in dishwater, clattering up against the sides of the sink.

The children would be arriving by boat the next day. I would be careful not to refer to them as "kiddo" or "sweetie." Careful not to bring up divorces, make outdated diagnoses of their mental health, justify past choices that had hurt them, open up wounds that had maybe healed.

The rain stopped. I could hear the doors of their bedrooms, even though they were firmly closed. My wife appeared at the end of the bed, removing her earrings. Her face, like the sea, was out of control with excitement.

I kissed her. The apple tree grew in the yard. The rain barrel spilled from the open top. The tide pulled against the rocks. I was feeling none of the anger I had carried for the last year and a half. I placed the word *why* on my table with my glasses and my paperback. I turned off the bedside light.

*

None of them let me carry their suitcases upstairs. They'd brought toys. They'd brought flowers. They'd brought the smell of the sea. They'd brought a cello case. One of the grandkids plays cello!

They ascended the staircase, which creaked like the stairs of a church.

It had been more than five hundred days, endless waves, and miles and miles by sea.

The rain held off. The first meal was finished. The stars had brushed their teeth.

Ghosts, no doubt waiting to re-form, had broken apart.

I kissed their faces, the dirty dishes. I kissed lampshades around the house.

My feet hurt, though we hadn't gone anywhere—

needle a hull's shadow over the start.

NOTES

Cold Enough for Snow is a novel by Jessica Au (New Directions Publishing, 2022).

"Better Than it Sounds in Real Life" riffs on a poem called "The Foley Artist's Apprentice" by Caitlin Doyle, which I encountered in the May 2012 issue of *The Atlantic*.

The first set of italicized lines in "C/G" are from an October 2020 interview with Adrianne Lenker that appeared on the music website pitchfork.com.

*

The long poem "The Minim" incorporates found text from *The Illustrated Dictionary of Musical Terms*, by Christopher Headington, The Bodley Head (Great Britain), 1980.

*

A number of the poems in the section "Two Rooms" approximate, reverse, erase and incorporate various elements of working translations I've been doing sporadically over the years from the poems of Spanish poet José Hierro. These poems can be found in their original language on pages 535, 60, 568 & 288 of *Poesías completas (1947-2002)*, José Hierro, Colección Visor de Poesía, Madrid.

The italicized lines from "Oh" contain lines from my own translation of Hierro's poem "Acelerando."

"Port of Call" is written after, and contains a line from, Hierro's poem "Caballero de otoño."

"The Music of Other Waves" takes its title from the last line of Hierro's poem "Para un esteta" and opens with a variation on a line from the same poem.

"Reversing the Tempo" flips the completed translation I'd done of Hierro's poem "Acelerando" from bottom line to top, blows it out into prose and changes every word. It remains distinctly haunted by the original.

The italicized line from "Luka Dončić" is taken from the essay "The Heresy of Zone Defense" by Dave Hickey, in his book *Air Guitar: Essays on Art and Democracy*, Art Issues Press, 1997.

ACKNOWLEDGEMENTS

This work would not have been completed without the assistance of a 2022 Creation Grant from artsnb.

Thank you to Janine Young, Silas White and everyone at Nightwood Editions. Thank you to Natalie Olsen for the gorgeous cover.

A few of these poems first appeared in a limited-edition chapbook called *The Cloud from All Sides* (Anstruther Press, 2021). Thanks to Jim Johnstone, editor.

"Clouds on a Drive" and "Small Talk" appeared previously in my mixed-genre collection *If It Gets Quiet Later On, I Will Make a Display* (the former with a slightly altered title). Thanks to Nightwood Editions for letting me use them here.

Thank you to Sue Sinclair and Matthew Gwathmey for reading the manuscript in its entirety, and to Rob Taylor and Raoul Fernandes for feedback on some early drafts of these poems.

Thank you to Sue, Abigail and Smoke—my family.

ABOUT THE AUTHOR

Photo credit: Kelly Baker Photography

Nick Thran's books include the mixed-genre collection *If It Gets Quiet Later On, I Will Make a Display* and three previous collections of poems. *Earworm* (Nightwood Editions, 2011) won the 2012 Trillium Book Award for Poetry. His poems have been anthologized in *Best Canadian Poetry* and *The Next Wave: An Anthology of 21st Century Canadian Poetry*. Nick lives on unceded Wolastoqey territory / Fredericton, New Brunswick, where he works as an editor and bookseller.